# Salvation For Your Unsaved Mom:

# 10 Things To Tell Your Mom Before She Dies

## By: Patrick Baldwin

# Table of Contents

# 1. Special Gift

Please Scroll to the Back of the Book for

A Special Gift

To Help You and Your Mom

**If You Would Like to Share Your Story with Us or Stay in Contact Our Contact**

**Information Can Be Found in the Back of the Book**

# Remember . . . .

*"All Things Are Possible With God"*

# 2. Dedication

This book is dedicated to my Mom with Love – Without You I Wouldn't Be Who I Am Today. I Thank God for Putting You In My Life to Help Lead and Guide Me Along Life's Journey. I hope to repay you now with this Book and return the Grace of God to You by Guiding You to the Only thing that Truly Matters.

This Book is also dedicated to all the single Mom's out there who have had to endure the hardships that a single parent so often has to deal with – Know You Are Appreciated & Loved!

## To My Mom:

You Never Gave Up On Me – Thank You

You Never pushed Religion on me – Thank You

You Never told me what to Believe – Thank You

You Gave me Time to be Self-Aware & Know Myself – Thank You

You Allowed Me to "Think for Myself & Learn from God"

~Thank You~

# 3. Forward

*To My Mom:*

This book represents my attempt to say what needed to be said while there is yet time to say it in hopes that you will come to the knowledge of the truth, repent of your sin, and accept and confess the Lord Jesus Christ. The sense of Urgency I have felt to put this book out cannot be understated. God has put within my Heart like never before a call to reach out to you one last time before eternity is a reality. I Love You so much Mom and I truly want the Best for You. I hope You will Consider the words of this Book and Act upon them before it's too late.

The Purpose of this Book is Ultimately A Call to Action by the Reader or Listener of this Book – God Says, Behold Now is the Acceptable Time for Salvation – Now!

This Book is intended to be a resource for fellow believers of Jesus Christ to use as more of a guideline than anything else (Every Situation is Different), to enable you with the tools necessary to start the conversation of Salvation, to motivate you with the desire to reach out to your mom – Understanding eternity is an ever approaching reality for all of us.

# 4. My Mom's Story

## My Mom's Story - The Evolution –

## A Brief Version

Mom's story may be similar to any single parent attempting to raise two sons without a father present. I'm not going to go into too much detail here just the general overview. Mom has never been one for listening to other people, on taking too much "crap" from those around her. She's always been a straight shooter and tells you like it is according to what she thinks. There's a phrase that we both got from her mom, "Don't ask me to tell you what you think if you don't want my honest opinion".

My has had her share of bad relationships, and a divorce with my father when I was around four. On numerous occasions I had to come to her aid in various ways. I have always been there trying to have her back in whatever way I could. I think this book may be a continuation of that same spirit.

Mom's routine was always to go to the local bar, VFW, or American Legion on her days off. Working a warehouse job for over 20 years takes its toll no doubt. So she would go there to socialize with her friends. She wasn't really a drinker or into drugs (Thank God), she just went there to hang out with her friends and relax from the day-to-day grind.

In 2005 when our daughter was born Mom became Nana and a change began in her. The hardness that was ever present began to soften to some degree, yet not completely. Mom suffers from

Diabetes, High Blood Pressure, and a few other medical conditions that affect her moods. When her sugars low – watch out . . . . .

Recently in the past year or two she began dating once again – someone she meet at the VFW. It was good to see her being treated with respect for once – bags being held for her, doors being opened etc. Hmmm did she finally find gentlemen to treat her right? As the relationship progressed I saw more of a change in her – She was in love, and at 64 – wow! God is truly awesome to provide someone like this for my mom at this stage in her life. Each and every step I was seeing God move in her life to soften her heart.

Yet it was just that – Her Heart – that would be the reason and motivation for the development of this Book. It was during this time where she started having issues with her heart that God put it on my heart to earnestly pray for her Salvation. As mom continued to have issues with her heart she was in and out of the hospital - long story short; she ended up being scheduled for surgery in late 2015. At the Hospital after she went back to be prepped for surgery, having my laptop with me I started to write down the chapters and outline of this book. I wanted to make sure I said what God wanted me to say before she died and time ran out. Life is short and so is Time – Seize the Moment Now Before both Run Out!

# 5. I Love You . . .

I Love You To Much NOT to Tell You the Truth . . . .

I love you for many reasons, but most of all I love you because you chose to let me live. When I was conceived you chose to take care of me by taking care of yourself so that I would have the best possible beginning.

I also love you because you provided a home for me, sacrificed your time, energy, and attention for me. You put your own needs and desires on standby so that mine could be fulfilled. You made me feel safe and secure.

You made me feel loved. You still do. Thank you.

But you aren't the only one who makes me feel loved. God makes me feel loved, too. He devotes his attention to my needs. He gives me security and safety in knowing he is always present. He chose you to be the one in whom I was formed. Most of all, however, he sacrificed His son Jesus. He did this so that I can have the hope of eternity with Him in heaven. For that and so much more, I love Him.

Mom, I love you so much that I want you to experience the love I have for God and the love He has for you, too. I want you to know Him personally; not just passively. I want you to experience the peace that comes from being His child. I want you to have the same hope of eternity in heaven that I do.

Why do I want you to have these things? Because I love you so much, that's why. I want the best for you—the best that can only be found in Jesus Christ.

Mom, it's not enough to be a 'good person'. It's not enough to treat people with compassion and to be a person of integrity. Oh, those things are enough for the world we live in, but this world and the life we are living are only temporary. No one lives forever here on earth, but everyone lives forever in the span of time we call eternity. The question is where? There are two choices. Heaven or Hell. That's it and God is the supreme judge—the one who will judge each and every one of us.

Thankfully, though, He didn't leave it up to us to figure out what He desires and expects of us in order to spend eternity with Him rather than in Hell. The Bible tells us exactly what He asks of us—and considering He allowed his son, Jesus, to die as a payment for *our* sins, it really isn't too much to ask of us at all.

So Mom, please take a few minutes to read the following scriptures. Read them and let the words speak to your heart. Please. I love you too much to not share this with you because I love you too much to not spend eternity with you and with God.

*For God so loved the world that he gave his one and only Son, that whosoever believes in him shall not perish but have everlasting life.*
*~John 3:16*

*Let us hear the conclusion of the whole matter: Fear God, and keep his commandments: for this is the whole duty of man. For God shall bring every work into judgment, with every secret thing, whether it be good, or whether it be evil. ~Ecclesiastes 12:13-14*

*Now when they heard this, they were pricked in their heart, and said unto Peter and to the rest of the apostles, Men and brethren, what shall we do? Then Peter said unto them, Repent, and be baptized every one of you in the name of Jesus Christ for the remission of sins, and ye shall receive the gift of the Holy Ghost. ~Acts 2:37-38*

# 6. Hope In God

As Long as there is Breath in Your Lungs there is Hope in God for Change . . .

In the Bible, we read about one of Jesus' disciples—a man by the name of Phillip. One day Phillip met an Ethiopian eunuch while he was walking on the road, the eunuch was sitting in his chariot reading. He was eager for Phillip to explain to him what he was reading. When the Ethiopian heard the Good News of salvation through Jesus, he didn't hesitate for a minute. He wanted to be baptized right then and there.

In the New Testament book of Acts, chapter 16, we read about the jailer who had been assigned to watch over Paul and Silas after they had been arrested for preaching about Jesus. But this didn't stop Paul and Silas. They preached and sang in prison so that everyone there could hear. Late that night, God sent an earthquake to shake the doors of the jail open and break off the chains around Paul and Silas' arms and legs. The jailer believed what they taught and was so amazed at what happened that he as well as his entire family were baptized when they heard the message of Salvation through Jesus from Paul and Silas.

But Jesus tells a parable (story) about a rich man who died and was sent to hell. When he got there and experienced the agony and pain that is hell, he cried out; begging to warn his family about what awaits them if they don't live a life of obedience to God. Jesus goes on to say that the man's request was denied because his family has the chance to hear and believe the Word of God on their own.

The message Jesus was sending by telling this story is this: as long as we are alive we have the opportunity to accept Jesus Christ as our Savior, but once we die, it is too late. There are no do-overs once we are gone from this life.

I want you to have the hope in God that I have.

I want you to have the hope that comes from knowing God is in control of your life if you will only let Him be. I want you to be able to enjoy life here on earth knowing that you are God's child and can receive the blessings He wants to give you after you confess, repent, and give yourself over to him through baptism and obedience to His Word. I want you to have the hope of God and for eternity with Him and know the joy that comes from standing with Him. I want you to know the peace that comes from having that hope; a peace that erases the fear of death.

I don't want to live once you are gone knowing that there is no hope for you and knowing we will not be spending eternity together. Please don't leave me to carry this burden on my heart. I want so badly to see you claim Jesus as your Savior before God and before men. I want us to spend the rest of our time together knowing our passing is not the end of our time together. Please, Mom, don't let death be the end of our being together.

*Trust in the Lord with all your heart and lean not on your own understanding; in all your ways acknowledge him and he will direct your paths. ~Proverbs 3:5-6*

*Be careful for nothing; but in everything by prayer and supplication with thanksgiving let your requests be made known unto God. And the peace of God, which passeth all understanding, shall keep your hearts and minds through Christ Jesus. ~Philippians 4:6-7*

*Whosoever therefore shall confess me before men, him will I confess also before my Father which is in heaven. ~Matthew 10:32*

*Even the youths shall faint and be weary, and the young men shall utterly fall: But they that wait upon the Lord shall renew their strength; they shall mount up with wings as eagles; they shall run, and not be weary; and they shall walk, and not faint. ~Isaiah 40:30-31*

*"The Lord is my portion," saith my soul, "therefore I will hope in him." ~Lamentations 3:24*

*Behold, the eye of the Lord is upon them that fear him, upon them that hope in his mercy.  ~Psalm 33:18*


*My soul fainteth for they salvation: but I hope in thy word. ~Psalm 119:81*


*Lord, I have hoped for they salvation, and done they commandments. ~Psalm 119:166*

# 7. People are Praying

Relationships are formed when people communicate with one another. You communicated your love for me by your words, actions, and attitudes. Did you know God does the same thing with us? And did you know we can talk back to God…and that he listens? It's true. It's called prayer.

Even if you think God has forgotten you, no one cares, or you have just given up, I want you to know people are praying for you right now and the power of Prayer is unstoppable through faith. God hears us when we pray and because He loves us He wants to honor (answer) our prayers when we pray for His will to be done.

What is his will? It's really very simple. God's will is that everyone everywhere to come to the knowledge of the truth in Christ Jesus and accept Him as their Savior.

Image that! Numerous people praying for God's will to be done in your life. They are praying that you will believe, confess your sins to God, repent (change from living on your own terms to living in obedience to God) and allow Jesus to save you from your sins and give you the gift of the Holy Spirit.

God had a plan for you even before you were born. He is just waiting for you to say "Okay, here I am. I'm ready to do things Your way, God." He isn't done with you yet. He's waiting for you to come to him. It's your choice to accept Christ as Savior or not, but I am praying you make the decision to do so. Others are praying for this, as well. Most of all, you need to know that God is waiting and listening for you to come to Him in prayer.

I pray for you each and every day. I pray for your health, your safety, and that you are blessed with happiness, solid relationships, financial peace of mind, and that you are able to enjoy your life. But most of all I pray for your salvation—that you accept Jesus and Savior.

I am not the only one praying for you, though. My church family is praying for you, as well. Please don't take offense to this fact or feel their prayers come from a sense of superiority or pity. These people are praying for you because they are my brothers and sisters in Christ and because they want you to become part of God's family, too.

Praying for others is something God calls us to do in the New Testament book of Philippians 4:6-7:  *Be careful for nothing; but in everything by prayer and supplication with thanksgiving let your requests be made known unto God. And the peace of God, which passeth all understanding, shall keep your hearts and minds through Christ Jesus.* Do you see? We are concerned for you and our concerns are to be put before God in prayer.

Prayer is real and powerful. Elijah prayed for the son of the widow of Zarephath to be raised back to life and he was. Elijah also prayed that God would show himself to be the One and Only God by sending fire from heaven and he did. Jonah prayed God's forgiveness from the belly of the fish and for a chance to be obedient. God forgave him and gave him another chance by causing the fish to spit Jonah from his mouth. Hannah poured her heart out to God in prayer for a child. He gave her Samuel and other children in the years that followed. Paul prayed for the life of Lydia to be restored and it was. Jesus prayed God's will be done before He went to the cross and it was.

I know you are thinking things like that don't happen today. And you are right…and wrong. God doesn't work in the same ways he did long ago, but He is the same yesterday, today, and forever. He is still living, active, and ever-present. He still does miracles every single day. Jesus is the living Word of God. He is able to do whatever He feels needs to be done. He is still in control. He still longs and needs to hear us speak to him and to speak back to us. So while there is still breath in your lungs there is still hope for you to know God and to experience the power of prayer. But prayer is about more than getting something from God. Prayer is about your relationship with God.

Prayer brings peace of mind. Prayer brings comfort. Prayer brings wisdom and resolution. Prayer brings forgiveness. Prayer brings hope and healing.

The prayers we are praying for you are for all of these. I love you, Mom, and I will never stop praying for you.

*Is any among you afflicted? let him pray. Is any merry? let him sing psalms. Is any sick among you? let him call for the elders of the church; and let them pray over him, anointing him with oil in the name of the Lord: And the prayer of faith shall save the sick, and the*

*Lord shall raise him up; and if he have committed sins, they shall be forgiven him. Confess your faults one to another, and pray one for another, that ye may be healed. The effectual fervent prayer of a righteous man availeth much. ~James 5:13-16*

*Likewise the Spirit also helpeth our infirmities: for we know not what we should pray for as we ought: but the Spirit itself maketh intercession for us with groanings which cannot be uttered. ~Romans 8:26*

*If we confess our sins, he is faithful and just to forgive us our sins and cleanse us from all unrighteousness. ~1st John 1:9*

*My voice shalt thou hear in the morning, O Lord; in the morning will I direct my prayer unto thee, and will look up. ~Psalm 5:3*

*For the eyes of the Lord are over the righteous, and his ears are open unto their prayers: but the face of the Lord is against them that do evil. ~1st Peter 3:12*

# 8. I'm Here for You

I'm here for you and so is Jesus - He will never leave you nor forsake you if you believe in your heart and confess with your mouth God raised Him form the Dead for with the Heart one believes onto Righteousness and with the mouth Confession is made unto Salvation.

You are not alone. I'm here for you; here to care for you as you need to be cared for.

I'm here for you; here to listen when you need someone to talk to.

I'm here for you; here to advise you when you are unsure of what to do.

I'm here for you; here to be your advocate and an extra pair of eyes and ears when you feel you aren't being listened to, seen, or respected.

I'm here for you; here to pray for you and share with you the truth of God's unconditional love for you and the hope of salvation through Jesus.

I'm here for you, but God is here for you in ways I cannot be.

We are not alone. God is here for you and me. He is everything I am for you and more. God is here for you and me the same way He was with the mighty men and women of faith in the Bible. The way He was with Abraham when Abraham was willing to sacrifice his own son if it was God's will.

God is here for you and me the same way He was with Esther when He put her in the position of being queen, which ultimately led to saving the entire Jewish race.

God is here for you and me the same way He was with Daniel when he boldly refused to comply with his captors' demands for his diet and when he was placed in a pit with lions because he refused to worship anyone but God.

God is here for you and me the same way He was with Joseph when he was sold by his brothers; ultimately leading to his position as second only to Pharaoh in Egypt (which allowed him to save his family from starvation).

God is here for you and me the same way He was with Joseph and Mary when they brought the Savior into the world and shielded Him from Herod's death-march.

God is here for you and me the same way He was with Nicodemus when he faithfully, but quietly followed Jesus; enabling him to retain his position within the Jewish hierarchy, which prevented Jesus from being arrested before it was time.

God is here for you and me the same way He was with Paul on all of his missionary journeys as he told the Good News of Jesus to everyone he could.

God is here for you and me the same way He was with everyone since the beginning of time who has lived and died seeking a personal relationship with Him.

God is here for you and me because He loves us and because it is His heart's desire that we are as personally interested in Him as He is in us.

Mom, I want you to know you are not alone and that as long as I live I will be here for you. I know I can never give to you as much as you've given me, but I want you to know that if I could I would. Mom, I have your back—I always have and always will. I want to share with you the love God has shown me so that you can see and experience it, too. We've been through so much together, so please, let's continue our life together into eternity with God.

*These things I have spoken unto you, that in me ye might have peace. In the world ye shall have tribulation: but be of good cheer; I have overcome the world. ~John 16:33*

*... "I will never leave thee nor forsake thee." ~Hebrews 13:5*

*But God commendeth his love toward us, in that, while we were yet sinners, Christ died for us. ~Romans 5:8*


*And we know that all things work together for good to them that love God, to them who are the called according to his purpose. ~Romans 8:28*

# 9. God Loves You. . . .

Mom, how much do you love me? Silly question, right? It's silly because there are really no words adequate for describing the love between a mother and her child. It's a love that just is. It's a love that happens from the heart and soul.

The love God has for you is the same—only better and with a greater intensity than you can comprehend. God loves you because you are. He created you in His image, so therefore He loves you because you are a part of Him.

I've said it before, but I'll say it again—more than anything. He can't help Himself. He created you so He loves you. He loves you so much that He was willing to sacrifice His son, Jesus on the cross in order that your sins can be forgiven…erased…forgotten. The love God has for you is like none other. God did this for you because the thought of you spending eternity in Hell rather than with Him breaks his heart. But just like you can't experience the warmth of a fire unless you are close enough to feel the heat it gives off, you can't experience the blessings of God's love unless you are close enough to receive them.

In order to get that closeness, you have to acknowledge God's love for you. This is done when you confess your sins, repent, and accept Jesus Christ as your Savior.

The Old Testament book of Genesis tells us that everything he created He looked at and said it was good. But when He created man (Adam and Eve) He told Jesus He was going to create them in OUR IMAGE. When He was done, God pronounced this element of His creation to be VERY good. In other words, we are God's greatest accomplishment.

Think about it like this: think about it from the viewpoint of me being your life's greatest accomplishment. After all, you gave birth to me, nurtured me, raised me, and loved me into adulthood. Hopefully you even look at me and say VERY good. So because you value me the way you do you treat me with all the TLC a guy could ask for and want what is best for me in all situations because that's what parents do for their kids. Or at least that's what they want to do for their kids.

What would happen if I wouldn't let you? What if I rejected your love and attention? What if I disassociated myself from you? How would you feel?

The way you would feel is how God feels about you right now (multiplied many times over). Your disassociation and rejection is breaking God's heart. The question I have for you now is why? Why would you want to do this to God? Why won't you let Him be the LORD of your life? Why won't you give yourself (and me) the assurance that we will spend eternity together?

*For God so loved the world that he gave his only begotten Son, that whosoever believes in him shall not perish but have eternal life.
~John 3:16*


*Behold, what manner of love the Father hath bestowed upon us, that we should be called the sons of God ~1ˢᵗ John 3:1*


*The Lord hath appeared of old unto me, saying, Yea, I have loved thee with an everlasting love.... ~Jeremiah 31:3*


*The Lord hath appeared of old unto me, saying, Yea, I have loved thee with an everlasting love ~Psalm 103:11*

*The Lord is merciful and gracious, slow to anger, and plenteous in mercy. ~Psalm 103:8*

# 10. The Only Way . . .

Do you remember the kid's game, Candyland®? It didn't matter whether you drew the card with peanut brittle, a lollipop, or cards with different colored squares on them, there was only one path to take you to King Kandy. Along the way you might get to skip a few (or a lot) of spaces. You might get stuck on the spaces with the black dots, or you may be so close to the end you can 'feel' it—only to draw the card with the peppermint sticks and have to start from the bottom again. But no matter what…there's only one path that takes you to the end.

The same thing is true when it comes to salvation—only your salvation is NOT a game and there is only one way in which you can be saved. The only one way to be saved by God is through His son, Jesus Christ. That's it. You cannot be nice enough, compassionate enough, give enough money to charity, or do enough good deeds in order to be saved. It is only by the blood of Jesus Christ and the grace and mercy of God the Father that you can have the hope of eternity in heaven.

You might be able to avoid some of the pitfalls of life such as financial hardships, serious illness, or the grief that comes from a failed marriage or rebellious children. Or you might have to trudge through some of these things; feeling as if you are forever getting knocked down and having to start over again. Either way, however, life starts with birth and ends in death for all of us. But what happens after death…that's what is really important.

Everyone is going to experience eternity. Eternity will either be spent with God in the heavenly home He has prepared for us or in Hell. I know I've already said that, but it's worth repeating because your eternity and where you spend it depends upon you knowing and accepting Jesus Christ as your Savior.

As frustrating as the game of Candyland® could be sometimes, life has even more frustrations, disappointments, and challenges. But unlike the game, we don't have to be at the mercy of the card we draw. We have a Savior and a loving Father God who is there for us. He is always ready to help us through the muck and mire of life here on earth so that when our life here is over, we can be with Him. But this can only happen if we put our faith and trust in Him now.

*Jesus saith unto him, I am the way, the truth, and the life: no man cometh unto the Father, but by me.  ~John 14:6*

*And now why tarriest thou? arise, and be baptized, and wash away thy sins, calling on the name of the Lord.  ~Acts 22:16*

*Not everyone that saith unto me, Lord, Lord, shall enter into the kingdom of heaven; but he that doeth the will of my Father which is in heaven.  ~Matthew 7:21*

*...Which sometime were disobedient, when once the longsuffering of God waited in the days of Noah, while the ark was a preparing, wherein few, that is, eight souls were saved by water. The like figure*

*whereunto even baptism doth also now save us (not the putting away of the filth of the flesh, but the answer of a good conscience toward God,) by the resurrection of Jesus Christ: Who is gone into heaven, and is on the right hand of God; angels and authorities and powers being made subject unto him.* ~1st Peter 3:20-22

# 11. Your Plan . . .

God created you with specific plans in mind for your life. He tells us so in the Old Testament book of Jeremiah. Let's look at a specific verse on the subject of the plan God has for your life…

*For I know the thoughts that I think toward you, saith the Lord, thoughts of peace, and not of evil, to give you an expected end.*
*~Jeremiah 29:11*

How do those words make you feel? Hopeful? Relieved? Scared? Indifferent? Defiant? Confused? Ready to know?

Chances are you feel a little bit of all of these. I know I have. I am thankful for God has a plan for me. I'm hopeful because I know I will receive God's blessings when I am obedient to Him. I'm relieved because of the comfort I get from knowing God is in control. I get scared and indifferent at times because I can't see the big picture the way God can. I've even been defiant at times—times when I wanted to do one thing but God obviously wanted something else. This can lead to confusion, but ultimately, I am ready to know and live the life God wants me to live because I know he knows what is best for me every day and in every way.

God knows what is best for you, too. Every day and in every way He knows what is best for you.

First and foremost He knows you will live the best life possible if you live it in Him. He created you to be with Him; to be His child. But because of sin, this can't happen until you accept the gift of forgiveness he gives through the sacrifice of his son, Jesus, on the cross. THIS is God's number one plan for you.

Secondly, God has specific plans for you in regards to what you do with your life. No, he's not in the business of pulling strings and orchestrating your every move like a puppeteer, but he created you to have talents and abilities which he wants you to use. When you do, you achieve a greater sense of satisfaction and self-worth. But he intends for you to use your talents and abilities in ways that honor him, too. For example, someone gifted with a strong business sense should conduct all business dealings with honesty, integrity, and with a heart that gives to those in need and with a sense of fairness and compassion toward those he or she does business with.

God's plan for you also includes being the one you come to for comfort in hard times, the one you praise and give credit to for the good things that happen in your life, and the one you come to for advice and counsel in all things.

Before you were even born God knew the person He would create and what He wanted for your life. The question is will you let him show you who that person is and how perfect His plan for your life is? I hope so because I want you to know the joy of living a saved and purposeful life in God.

*Hope deferred maketh the heart sick: but when the desire cometh, it is a tree of life.*

*~Proverbs 13:12*

*The Lord is the portion of mine inheritance and of my cup: thou maintainest my lot. The lines are fallen unto me in pleasant places; yea, I have a goodly heritage. ~Psalm 16:5-6*

*And why take ye thought for raiment? Consider the lilies of the field, how they grow; they toil not, neither do they spin: And yet I say unto you, That even Solomon in all his glory was not arrayed like one of these. Wherefore, if God so clothe the grass of the field, which today is, and tomorrow is cast into the oven, shall he not much more clothe you, O ye of little faith? Therefore take no thought, saying, What shall we eat? or, What shall we drink? or, Wherewithal shall we be clothed? For after all these things do the Gentiles seek:) for your heavenly Father knoweth that ye have need of all these things. But seek ye first the kingdom of God, and his righteousness; and all these things shall be added unto you. ~Matthew 6:28-33*

*For thou hast possessed my reins: thou hast covered me in my mother's womb. I will praise thee; for I am fearfully and wonderfully made: marvelous are thy works; and that my soul knoweth right well. My substance was not hid from thee, when I was made in secret, and curiously wrought in the lowest parts of the earth. Thine eyes did see my substance, yet being unperfect; and in thy book all my members were written, which in continuance were fashioned, when as yet there was none of them. ~Psalm 139:13-16*

# 12. Under Heaven

One of the most difficult things for people to understand is the fact that everything happens for a reason. They say things like:

- "If God was real, He wouldn't let that happen."
- "If God was the loving God you say He is, He wouldn't let a child die."
- "There is no such thing as a miracle. That was luck (or fate)."

The truth of the matter, however, is this: Everything happens for a reason and there is a time for everything to happen. This includes the events of your life, too.

Sometimes things happen as a result of the poor choices we make. Sometimes things happen because of the good choices we make and sometimes things happen because of God's power and miraculous intervention.

The Old Testament book of Exodus tells us that God allowed the Israelites to live in bondage in Egypt for 430 years. That's a long time to let the people you call your children suffer, but God was waiting for Moses. He knew Moses was the one who to lead them out of Egypt; the one able to handle their attitudes of complaining and disobedience in spite of all God did for them.

The Bible is filled with accounts that show God's perfect timing. From providing the sacrificial lamb to Abraham 'just in the nick of time' to choosing Mary to be the mother of the Savior and Jesus' death, burial, and resurrection, everything happens in just the right time to bring God's plan to fruition.

Like any good parent, God doesn't leave anything to chance. That's why He placed it upon my heart to write this book—because it was time to get serious about sharing the message of salvation with you. He knows the time is right for you to hear and receive the Word and to come to Him. The question is do *you* know the time is right?

As you read through the following verses found in the Old Testament book of Ecclesiastes, I want you to think about your life—the times when you laughed, cried, fought, enjoyed peace, celebrated, grieved, and did everything else God appointed times for you to do. Can you see God in these times? Will you see God in these times?

*To everything there is a season, and a time to every purpose under the heaven: A time to be born, and a time to die; a time to plant, and a time to pluck up that which is planted; A time to kill, and a time to heal; a time to break down, and a time to build up. A time to weep, and a time to laugh; a time to mourn, and a time to dance; A time to cast away stones, and a time to gather stones together; a time to embrace, and a time to refrain from embracing; A time to get, and a time to lose; a time to keep, and a time to cast away; A time to reap, and a time to sew; a time to keep silence, and a time to speak; A time to love, and a time to hate; a time of war, and a time of peace.*
*~Ecclesiastes 3:1-8*

*And let us not be weary in well doing: for in due season we shall reap, if we faint not. ~Galatians 6:9*


*And we know that all things work together for good to them that love God, to them who are the called according to his purpose. ~Romans 8:28*

# 13. Perfect Timing . . .

Taking a cake out of the oven before it is done leaves you with a gooey-centered almost cake. But if you leave it in the oven too long, you end up with a cake that is dry, crusty, and one no one will eat.

Pulling into the garage before the door is all the way up, well, we all know what happens if you do that. But if you wait until the door is all the way up, you can drive right in, park your car and all is as it should be.

In both situations, timing is everything. The same is true when it comes to accepting Jesus Christ as your Savior. Taking this life-changing and life-giving step isn't something you should do under pressure, or because everyone else around you is doing so. It isn't even something to do because I want you to or because you want to make me happy. Accepting Christ as your Savior is something you do because YOU are ready to say, "I am a sinner. I need God's forgiveness. I want to give my life to Him and spend eternity in Heaven with God".

Throughout the pages of this book I've tried to show you why and how God's love is the only thing worth holding on to…worth living for. Not even the love we share as mother and son comes anywhere close to being comparable to the love we can experience as being God's child.

Have you 'heard' what my words and the words of the Bible have been saying? Do you understand that God's love is unconditional, that there is power in prayer, that He has a plan for your life, that in order to receive His blessings you have to be close enough to Him to realize them, and that the only way to God is through Jesus? If you do, then now is the time. Now is the perfect time to accept the gift of forgiveness and salvation through Jesus Christ. Will you?

*Study to shew thyself approved unto God, a workman that needeth not to be ashamed, rightly dividing the word of truth.   ~2nd Timothy 2:15*

*If we say that we have no sin, we deceive ourselves, and the truth is not in us. If we confess our sins, he is faithful and just to forgive us our sins, and to cleanse us from all unrighteousness.*

*~1st John 1:8-9*

*Then Peter said unto them, Repent, and be baptized every one of you in the name of Jesus Christ for the remission of sins, and ye shall receive the gift of the Holy Ghost   ~Acts 2:38*

# 14. Conclusion

*To My Mom*:

Throughout this Book I have attempted to appeal to you on many different levels with the Hope in God that His Spirit will touch your Heart along the way, giving you the understanding you need to make the one decision on earth that has eternal consequences. I hope and continue to pray that you will not be as stubborn in this as you have in other things throughout your life – play time is over mom, its time to get serious about where you're going after you die. Just believing is not enough – you have to confess Jesus to those around you. Jesus said that if you confess him before men He will also likewise confess you to His Father in Heaven.

Part of Salvation is this confession of Jesus Christ – The Scriptures indicate that with the heart one believes onto righteousness and with the mouth confession is made unto Salvation – Another words if you believe it, you got to speak it.

Mom You have struggled and suffered so much in this life . . . we won't go into why, it's irrelevant at this point but that is nothing to what awaits you without Jesus Christ in your heart, without accepting Him as your personal Lord and Savior.  I would ask that you accept Him into your heart for me, so I would not have the sorry and grief of your passing knowing that you continue to suffer even more in Hell; However, that will not work for God, for God knows your heart, He knows your mind – You have to do it because you know you need Him, because You want to, because the Spirit of God is Calling you to – No because of Me.

If you decide to you want to make that next step please see the page "God's Gift"

***To Those Reading This Book:***

I'd like to tell those reading this book that the story ends well and Mom became a Born-Again Christian but honestly the story continues. However, its Important to do our part to share the hope and love that only comes from having a personal relationship with Jesus Christ – Don't put off tomorrow what you can do today – Let Your Mom know how much you love and appreciate her despite whatever circumstances or dynamics you currently find your relationship.

# 15. God's Gift
~The Special Gift~

*God has a Gift for You!*

## Plan of Salvation:

There is no formal " prayer of salvation" as many churches would have you believe, God's word is very clear – there is only one way to get to the Father in heaven and that is through Jesus Christ (John 14:6).  Jesus says that you must be born again to enter into heaven (John 3:3-5).

Salvation is simply the first step in building an open & honest relationship with God.  We all have sinned and fall short every day, but there is Hope in Jesus Christ – Just cry out to God in sincerity and honesty for forgiveness asking Him to Save you, Sanctify you, and fill you with His Holy Spirit – Ask for His will to be done in your life on earth as it is in Heaven – That's it, now just keep it real with God.

**A Warning:**

The Christian walk is not an easy life on the surface. The word of God says that we will be hated in all the world for Christ namesake (Matt. 24:9). The Bible says that in the last days are enemy prevail against us until Christ returns to save us (Dan 7:21, 22). Furthermore, we must endure hardship as a good soldier of Jesus Christ (2 Tim 2:3) – yet we are never alone in this, God promises us that He will never leave us nor forsake us if we believe in him (Matt.28:20).

In everything we go through we have the peace & joy of God which surpasses all understanding (Philp. 4:6-8) The Bible declares, "For I consider the sufferings of this present time are not worthy to be compared with the glory which shall be revealed in us. (Rom 8:18). However, in all these things we are more than conquerors through Jesus Christ (Rom. 8:37)

# 16. Stay In Contact

Our Contact Information

Contactus@acdainc.org

# Please Visit Our Website At:

http://acdainc.org

We also Greatly Appreciate You Signing Up For Our Mailing List and Providing a Good Rating for This Book. If You or Your Family have been touched by this book please let us know by dropping us a line through our website.


Thanks Again for Reading


God Bless!

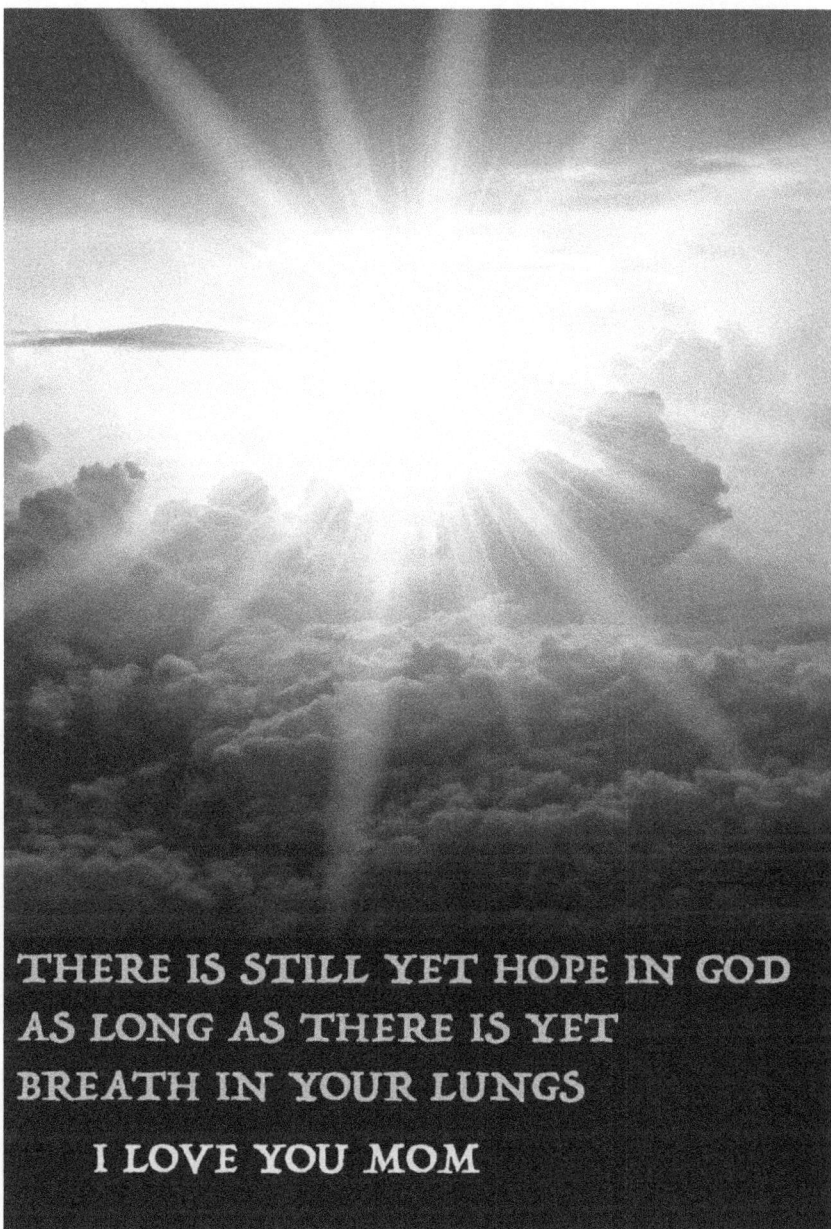

THERE IS STILL YET HOPE IN GOD
AS LONG AS THERE IS YET
BREATH IN YOUR LUNGS

I LOVE YOU MOM

www.ingramcontent.com/pod-product-compliance
Lightning Source LLC
Chambersburg PA
CBHW021921040426
42448CB00007B/853